The GQ Mugging Inquest

A Study in Masculine Culture

Dustcover

The GQ Mugging Inquest is a study in masculine culture, specifically the art of bonding conversation between African-American men of the generation that came of age in the 1960's and 70s.

From early 2013 through late 2014, the author, an urban violence researcher and novelist, visited one Northeast Baltimore bar where a handful of middle-aged men gathered to speak of sports, their work day, the current news, and of their youth. The GQ Mugging Inquest is his impression of their interesting, entertaining, and ultimately manly, art of conversation.

Key Words: masculinity, manhood, modernity, black studies

The GQ Mugging Inquest

The GQ Mugging Inquest

Books by James LaFond

Nonfiction

The Fighting Edge, 2000
The Logic of Steel, 2001
The First Boxers, 2011
The Gods of Boxing, 2011
All Power Fighting, 2011
When You're Food, 2011
The Lesser Angles of Our Nature, 2012
The Logic of Force, 2012
The Greatest Boxer, 2012
Take Me to Your Breeder, 2014
The Streets Have Eyes, 2014
Panhandler Nation, 2014
The Ghetto Grocer, 2014
American Fist, 2014
Don't Get Boned, 2014
Alienation Nation, 2014
In The Chinks of The Machine, 2014
How the Ghetto Got My Soul, 2014
Saving the World Sucks, 2014
Taboo You, 2014
The Fighting Life, 2014
Narco Night Train, 2014
Into the Mountains of Madness: in [3 volumes], 2014
Incubus of Your Sacred Emasculation, 2014
Breeder's Digest, 2014
The Third Eye, 2015
Modern Agonistics, 2015
By the Wine Dark Sea, 2015
The Pale Usher, 2015
The Third Eye, 2015

Fiction

Astride the Chariot of Night, 2014
Sacrifix, 2014
Rise, 2014
Motherworld, 2014
Planet Buzzkill, 2014
Fruit of The Deceiver, 2014
Forty Hands of Night, 2014
Black and Pale, 2014
Daughters of Moros, 2014
Darkly, 2014
Fat Girl, 2015
Hurt Stoker, 2015
Poet, 2015
Triumph, 2015
Winter, 2015
The Spiral Case, 2015
Hemavore, with Dominick Mattero, 2015
Yusuf of the Dusk, 2015
Mantid, 2015
RetroGenesis: Day 1, with Erique Watson, 2015

Sunset Saga Novels

Big Water Blood Song, 2011
Ghosts of the Sunset World, 2011
Beyond the Ember Star, 2012
Comes the Six Winter Night, 2012
Thunder-Boy, 2012
The World is Our Widow, 2013
Behind the Sunset Veil, 2013
Den of The Ender, 2013
God's Picture Maker, 2014
Out of Time, 2015
Seven Moons Deep, 2015

For Ted, my teacher in such matters

Contents

Where Men Speak 9

How Long Does it Take a Dying City to Eat
$3.50? 11

    The Traffic Stop 12

    Paying it Forward 13

    Conclusion 16

The GQ Mugging Inquest, with Testimony from
The Floyd Money, Mayo Sandwich, Strange
Coochy & Black Superman Inquests 21

    The Way of Men 23

    A Manly Den 25

    The Floyd Money Inquest 27

    The Mayo Sandwich Inquest 30

    Subject: William, A.K.A. Black Superman 33

    The Strange Coochy Inquest 36

    The Black Superman Inquest 37

    Subject: Quintin L. Tates 39

    The GQ Mugging Inquest 41

    A House Divided 47

Appendices 49

On The Steps 50

    Quinn's Walk 54

What Awaits the Man Who Fails to Find His Way:
Mo Coffee 58

   The Heartless Blogger 58

   Beyond the Ghetto? 59

   Mo Coffee 60

"In this world, shipmates, sin that pays its way can travel freely, and without a passport; wheras Virtue, if a pauper, is stopped at all frontiers."

-Herman Melville, Moby Dick

Where Men Speak

Confessions of An Amateur Ethnographer

In the winter of 2013 I was invited to a banquet for martial arts people. I did not know many of these people and was not sure what my function would be. It turned out my function was to vet a fighter and drink tequila with the host—so a good night was had by all, except for the fighter I exposed as wanting.

Next door was a non-descript bar over top of which I had rented the couch in a rooftop apartment in 1981 when I first moved to Baltimore. The bar was owned by a pro football player named Timmy who my Uncle Fred had coached in college—and I had no idea about that until last month, a good ten years after Timmy passed.

I noticed that the bar served a mixed-race clientele who self segregated and tended to about 50 years of age. People this age have stories to tell. Also, the blacks would, in many cases, remember moving up from Georgia and the Carolinas in the 'Great Migration.' This was important to me as I had just outlined the novel Hurt Stoker, which was set in Maryland in an alternate reality where the Confederacy won the Civil War. In listening to these older men—the eldest of which, Mister Al, was a former employee of mine—tell their tales great and small, I would be able to check my dialogue for authenticity. And then I saw the Floyd Money Inquest and was hooked on these old fellas; a likeable bunch of working men who had mostly spent time in college, did not drink for effect, argued about sports at the drop of a beer coaster, and discussed literature as well.

I began sitting at the 'fifty yard line' the right place for a race traitor to sit in a mixed-race sports bar. But the whites up front—nice as they might be— only talked sports unless compelled under duress to do otherwise.

Eventually, among a handful of the older black patrons I began to notice traces of an old European tradition from the Colonial Era, the heated discussion circle where men of action and men of letters tested each other's knowledge and character as well.

After my first brief stop for a National Boh draft and a shot of Captain Morgan I would have cause to return, and be glad I did. Many younger suburban readers might only understand a bar as a place to go, at night or on weekends, to get drunk, watch a major sports event, or meet a hopefully loose woman. But the neighborhood urban bar serves those needs only in the breach. Primarily, the urban American bar is a place where the weary, but not yet broken, working man, stops to forget what he can with the help of a drink, and remember what he must with the help of a friend.

How Long Does it Take a Dying City to Eat $3.50?

Harm City Lite: Sunday May 5, 2013

At 11:45 this morning I headed out to the school to put in some training and do some janitorial work. As the bus banked in and I boarded the driver held up her hand, and told me the meter was not accepting fares today. I thanked her and headed to the back.

I made my connection in plenty of time, had ten minutes to kill. It was now 12:14. A motorist with a handicapped tag was pulled over in the bus stop lane by a county cop. The motorist was not some oppressed youth about to fight for being profiled, but a middle-aged man with his wife, or informal equivalent.

The Traffic Stop

I could have hoofed it to the next stop. But really how long could this take? The cop is already writing the citation, and the bus will soon be able to pull over, so I sit, and observe.

Another cop pulls up and talks to the cop, and the driver.

The first cop talks to the driver and then comes around to have a separate conversation with the passenger, who apparently owns the vehicle and is the handicapped one.

A third cop pulls up—it is a traffic jam now. That cop talks to the two occupants, and then has a separate consultation with the driver. He then talks to the other two cops, each at their own vehicle.

The first cop produces a second citation and talks to all four parties again. I stop reading and start listening.

This vehicle has been flagged for long-term uninsured status by the state MVA, and the cops have been sent to pull the tags! Each cop, in his and her turn, have had the same subdued and congenial conversation with each occupant of the vehicle, and it is now 12:34. Hopefully the bus is five minutes off so I can get to the next stop, because it will not pull over here.

Now a tow truck shows up. The driver, a very unsympathetic looking fellow who I could imagine playing the heavy in a B-movie, now has a conversation with a cop, then the driver, than another cop...

There is no bus in sight so I start hoofing it. Then I hear the bus and begin to sprint. It is 200 yards to the stop. I can do it! The bus pulls over with 50 yards to go, and the elderly passengers take some time getting off, and I'm there. Unfortunately the bus driver does not look my way before pulling off. I wave, and then think about yelling, but am reminded how much yelling hurts that old groin injury and just let it go and walk.

Paying it Forward

I make it to the school a little late, put in my training, and leave at 3:00 p.m.. I still have my $3:50 and will not really need a ticket. So I decide to walk the few miles to the next line and just spend $2 to cover the $1.60 fare, and spend the $1.50 on a draft at a bar on the way home.

I wait at the stop with a stuffed-animal street vender, with a sack full of stuffed beasts strapped to his back, and hanging from his apparel. The bus pulls up, I board, and the meter is jammed, so I ride for free. This reminded me of how my fighter Curtis used to have trouble making weight when he took the bus. You see, so many Baltimore area busses have non-functioning meters that he regularly ended up getting home from the gym with at least $2 dollars that he had not planned on having. He lived right next door to a McDonalds, "and that's two sandwiches on the dollar menu Mister Jimmy!"

In honor of Curtis I decide to pay my uncollected bus fare forward. I am thirsty, am feeling old, so want to do something defiantly unhealthy that would maintain the three inches of armor that is currently shielding my pristine six-pack from damage. A draft it will be.

That counted out the biker bar, since they had no draft beer as a means of keeping microbrew nerds and black dudes from patronizing their heavy metal den of thieves.

The bar across the street is closed, the single patron's liver having apparently failed.

I enter the bar up the street. The ball game is on, which is perfect because I'm writing Hurt Stoker tomorrow. Whiff Gleason, the main character, is a former baseball player. There is also no one at the bar, which is nice, since the guys that are usually here are pretty loud and drugged up, this being the stoner bar. Unfortunately, Terry, the big-headed Frankenstein monster of barkeeps, is asleep, on the bar, snoring away.

The black bar next door is open, but the lights are out and I see no one at or behind the bar. Either someone is having sex with the barmaid or the place is being robbed, so I head home, and get my butt in this chair at 4:11 p.m.

Now it just occurred to me that I have not been able to pay my bus fare forward. It has also occurred to me that if I go down the street to the mixed-race alcoholic classic rock/NFL bar, and am unable to get a cheap draft there, than I have a vastly improbable story on my hands. I am fantasizing right now about a journey across town—maybe on buses without functional meters—to bar after bar whose bar-back called out and the barmaid does not know how to change a keg. This could be my break, an article in Rolling Stone!

In reality it is most likely that my adventure will merely consist of a cheap beer in an improperly washed mug as I sit between the old white hippy who looks like Roger Daltrey and plays Who songs on the juke box constantly, and the black dudes discussing their game bets while the rednecks up front [they sit there so they only have to waddle ten feet to get outside and smoke] commit brain cell genocide.

Well, I'm up for an adventure, and will hopefully get home at 3:00 a.m. with my conclusion.

James 4:48 p.m., heading out to pay it forward.

Conclusion

As best I can remember I'm a hundred years old and lost!

Okay, back up.

I just got in and it is 11:30. Yes, I am completely smashed—grammatical inebriation dispensation evoked.

The weather was very nice. So, on the way to the bar I was entertained by a ghettocross rider; a young guy in sweats illegally riding a dirt bike in violation of every traffic law he can violate, even driving against traffic. The cops no longer chase these guys for reasons beyond my knowledge, though I suppose their inability to catch these daredevils is a factor.

I entered the local NFL bar and discovered it was the local schizophrenic sports bar: with the MLB on the high definition up front for the white dudes who are completely annihilated; an NHL game on one screen for the vacant looking bearded guy in the corner; and the NBA on the two screens in the back for the five black dudes who are arguing over honey nut cheerios, cunnilingus and smacking down white European basketball players...

By 5:55 p.m. I had bought two National Bohemian drafts for $1.75 a piece and was now paid forward and spiraling into the abyss.

I quizzed the baseball coach who dropped by to see an inning.

The barmaid called out, but the bar-back was dragooned into keeping the place open, and was spending five minutes making sure that I did not get suds but a 5.4% alcohol buzz.

My Negro League ball player protagonist led me into a conversation with William, a former rec. council coach in numerous sports who explained to me the bio mechanics of batting to right field, and the social mechanics of body punching and African American street life.

The local hooker with spiked platform earrings hovered around as the stumble bum white drunks who were already annihilated when I showed up at 5:10 p.m. faded into the evening.

William turned out to be a great interview and we started watching fight replays on the overhead screen and on his smart phone. Richard, a New York man who played minor league ball for 13 years, showed up and gave us the update on the latest Floyd Mayweather fight, which he claims Floyd should have lost.

The GQ Mugging Inquest

Richard and Spike Lee—I think it was Spike Lee—talked for hours about boxing and about African American history until only Richard was left...

I bought Richard a drink and he, with his very sheik watch and jewelry, reminded me to button up my polo shirt to keep up appearances...

It was late and Richard and I were walking home together since he lives three blocks past me. Richard, at six foot and one-sixty—as I guessed on the nose, was just as uncomfortable with me knowing his weight as he was with the fact that he and I lived on the same street. He was having trouble walking because he had been shot in the leg some years ago, and because we drank too much cheap beer, so I kept an eye on him so that my interview did not get hit by a car. That would be unseemly you know.

He looked at my collar and noted that I could be respectable if only I always buttoned up, then I pulled him out of the street onto the sidewalk as a car approached and pointed to my legs, "Richard, I'm wearing black sweats underneath of black cargo shorts with brown work boots—that is irredeemable man!"

The GQ Mugging Inquest

He laughed and staggered out into traffic, saying, "Hey man, you are way too funny."

We then walked by the house where I rent the room from the karate guy who leaves the doors unlocked so he can beat up any intruders Chuck Norris like. I was worried about Richard getting hit by a car. So I pulled him out of traffic again and told him, "This is as far as I go."

He then pulled down his fly to water the neighbor's untrimmed bushes that force pedestrians to walk on the curb or in the gutter while a Hum-V rumbled by, and I was out of there…

Harm City got my money in the end.

What is the answer to the question that is the title?

After deducting the one hour I spent writing the first segment, it took six hours for Baltimore to take $3.5 of my money. But she was having a bad day, and after she got warmed up, she, like a housewife who has finally finished her morning coffee and realized there was still something in your wallet, took $12 more in the same timeframe.

Over and out at 12:22 am 5/6/2013…

The GQ Mugging Inquest, with Testimony from The Floyd Money, Mayo Sandwich, Strange Coochy & Black Superman Inquests

For the past 2 years I have been socializing with a number of black men from the generation ahead of me. These men average 60 years of age, all have a background in scholastic sports, most have university degrees, and half currently coach sports. One is a cop, and I try not to hold it against him. I have spilled a lot of ink—well, it is spraying toner now—writing about my interactions with young urban black men of the two generations behind me, largely for a white suburban and rural readership which tends toward those two age groups.

I have gone on record as describing myself as 'the last black man in Baltimore' to the howls of disapproval of liberal whites. I say this largely because I now behave, in my 'reverse retirement mindset' very much like the defiant twenty-something black man of 1975—never mind that I'm a 51 year old cracker looking at the yawning cultural chasm of 2015.

Oddly enough my black fighters didn't seem to mind this claim, as I remind them of their uncles from the 1960s and 1970s; who came of age when it was police policy to beat the shit out of random black men just to set a certain tone; who reached maturity in an age when young black men needed to compete in sports just to get a decent education; who actually lived much of the inequity that the young black hoodlums and hood rats of today claim as their burden; though it is nothing to them but a vast cow of displaced guilt to be milked.

Over the past year I have listened and watched, and talked a little, to the last generation of black men in this city that deserve to be called Men, just as the last generation of white men that was collectively worth the masculine honorific came of age in the 1950s.

Blacks entered mainstream American consumer life [which did not begin in earnest until after WWII] a generation later than whites, so seem to be that far behind in the process of emasculation. In the 1990s white bots [that is a typo but I'm keeping it] started staying home into middle age living off of mom as they played video games. Now black boys are accelerating the process by living off their baby's mom.

So, before they are extinct how do real men interact, just in case the feminists and angry man children out there are curious?

The Way of Men

I will use Jack Donovan's Way of Men *‘**The Primitive Math Of Violence**’* as a field handbook. God only knows that I am at enough of a disadvantage without a degree in sociology or anthropology. The last thing I need to do is compound that by using a guide written by some liberal babysitting drone or feminist mantrap.

In his seminal work Jack defined 4 masculine traits that define men for men, and by which men rate each other in the primal meat-ripping way of life, and hopefully might again someday after the Momocracy fails due to a facelift gone wrong or some other cosmetic disaster:

23

1. Strength

2. Courage

3. Mastery

4. Honor

It goes without saying that you don't achieve #4 without a good score in at least one of the three prerequisites. I will use this guide in my attempt to decode the various 'inquests' that constitute the ongoing manhood rites I have witnessed at the Mixed Race Sports Bar.

Note: Mainstream postmodern America only regards Mastery as a virtue. Strength is regarded as an unfair advantage of men over otherwise equal women, Courage as stupidity, and a vigorously applied sense of Honor as insanity. In street parlance, postmodern life is all about being slick, about being the smart person who games the system. A single virtue value system such as this is what you get when a materialistic society evolves to its apex.

A Manly Den

The bar is a masculine matrix. Women tend bar, and sometimes come as the guests of men. Sometimes they come alone or in pairs, to meet men. The minority white clientele are all smokers and sit by the front door. They are mostly working class and mostly uneducated, with even a reading of the sports page beyond their ken.

The majority black clientele of this white owned bar—which was founded by a pro football player who my Uncle Fred used to coach in college—do not smoke and favor the back of the bar as it gives easy access to the pool tables and is a better venue for conversation as there are three seating angles.

Although the median age is 55, a few young men— both white and black—congregate around the poker machines in the late afternoon.

For people such as myself who rent rooms, or for married men who need a break from the job or the wife, this is a nice place to meet for socializing. The conversation is commonly centered on sports, with an expert on every stool. This is the best thing about sports in this country, is that it provides a common ground for people of different races to converse passionately without acrimony.

However, once one gets beyond sports, there is no conversing with the whites, who generally drink for effect and read little. The few literary minded whites who frequent the bar sit with the blacks. Two of these men [William and Quinn] tackle annual reading lists. To a person like myself or Quinn who rent rooms, the bar provides a common space for reading, and for other men an escape from the banal bleating of women.

This past Tuesday night as I stood along the rail wall reading Quinn's newsletter, which he photocopies and passes out for free at Church, work [he is a physical education teacher at City College], the barber shop, and the bar, a woman walked in. As she noticed Quinn passing a newsletter to one of the manual labor class of black men who come here after work to hang out with the more educated men, she looked at the document and said, "Oh, somebody done died?"

Quinn scrunched his brows into a scowl of disdain as he explained it was a newsletter, and this ghetto representative went on her way, apparently not having seen a non glossy document with a photocopy of a man in a basketball uniform [LaBron James] that was not a homemade funeral program honoring a young man having met an untimely end.

The man—seemingly a construction worker by his hands and clothes—gladly accepted the latest edition of Quinn's sports newsletter and bought Quinn a drink. Quinn said, "You didn't have to do that, the newsletter is free."

The man responded, "Sure I do. I come here because of you. If you didn't come here this wouldn't be a bar, but just a place where people drink."

Quinn seemed shocked, so I targeted him for a review when he would be deep into his cups so that I might better help him, for Hawk had assigned me the task of rehabilitating Quinn in the wake of the disastrous 'GQ Mugging Inquest' of which he was the subject.

The Floyd Money Inquest

It was a Saturday night about a 18 months ago, perhaps 8:00 p.m. the whites upfront where staggering out drunk—all except the giant bearded hillbilly—and the remaining patrons were sitting for the Floyd Money Inquest. I had yet to speak with any of these men. I did note with a sense of good will that as the drunken whites left two of the larger older black men were offering to walk them home in the wake of all of the black youth muggings over the preceding months. I was sure now, as I stood along the side wall, that I had chosen the best place to study urban culture, as most of the patrons do not drink for effect as did those of the other neighborhood bars, all of which also proved to be highly segregated.

On my side of the bar sat a shrill, stocky man with his wife, shouting the praises of welterweight champ Floyd Money, of his 'gangster manipulation' of the Black versus Latino boxing race politics, and his 'non-losing' perfect record preserving method of boxing.

In most such inquests the entire bar gangs up on the off opinion in a kind of test, a rite of masculinity. These conversations, if had by whites, would involve two debating teams, or two debaters and two cheering sessions. These men, however, conduct themselves more like rich 19th Century white aristocrats, with the odd man expected to defend his unpopular opinion against all comers, like Richard F. Burton defiantly expounding on his gnostic vision of God against a room full of Anglican snobs.

However, in this inquest, there was a lead prosecutor, a dark slouch-shouldered man with cannonball biceps and a bowling ball dome of a head who had the look of a boxer, and by the tone with which he disparaged Floyd Money for being 'nothing but a run and hug chump' was once a fighter who had chased more than one 'point scoring coward' around the ring.

This Floyd Money Inquest reached the level of anger, as the former boxer finally dismissed the Floyd Money advocate for 'getting all caught up in the money and popularity bullshit' and forgetting what 'a boxer was supposed to be—a fighter, a man who brings it!'

The Inquisitor damned Floyd Money, and by extension his fan, for forgetting the importance of Strength and Courage, and relying on Mastery alone to attain Honor.

I approached the former boxer with a series of notes on the back of a business card concerning some old time fighters who are generally overlooked. He was fascinated, quizzed me on my boxing background, and when he found out I was a writer and a coach, told me not to miss an opportunity to speak on 'the sweet science' any time I was in.

This man goes by the name of Hawk, and seems to be the most respected man in the bar by a long shot, often serving as the judge of disputes and the lead prosecutor at formal inquests. He is the only patron I have seen tell other patrons that they had had too much to drink and need to moderate their behavior. Hawk has a warm body check handshake, meant to check your muscle tone and balance as much as a welcome, passes up few opportunities to buy me a drink, and tends to nominate me as a walking sourcebook.

The Mayo Sandwich Inquest

This past winter, the tall deep voiced patron, who stops in irregularly and is a ringer for Michael Jordan, was conducting an inquest of a very defensive Subject. This other man was timid, and bookish in a physical sense, but was fiercely argumentative. He had made a point on pronouncing a word and the tall Inquisitor called into question his 'blackness' making sure to turn and apologize to me for "getting racial up in here. But this shit is serious."

This point had to do with 'blackness' or being 'a real black man' being contingent on growing up poor, and hard, and preferably in the South, and knowing a life of austerity alien to the young African Americans of today. Finally, as the tall dark Inquisitor had the pretentious little man reeling before the men who seconded his every point and looked askance at the Subject, he swooped in for the kill.

"Everyone that came up hard knows you ain't a real black man unless you've eaten a mayonnaise sandwich! Now tell me you've eaten a mayo sandwich!"

The Subject nervously took a sip of beer and looked to all sides with darting eyes as the Inquisitor took a real black man roll call.

"Any man here that has eaten a mayo sandwich raise your hand!"

The GQ Mugging Inquest

One by one, as the man who had been found wanting squinted and frowned, the hands were raised. Finally in his defense, as all hands but his were raised, he said, "Yeah, but half of ya'all probably ate Helmans or Kraft at least. My mother bought that store brand stuff!"

The tall Inquisitor leaned back on his stool and rocked from side to side, racking his mind for the off brand mayo of his youth. "I know the label. It had this beige color and black lettering—with the name in red. It was some shit, the cruddiest shit you eva ate. I jus' cain't remember the brand."

The Subject was coming back, bouncing off of the ropes of rejection. "That's because you but visited your mamma probably but once a year to go to the beach and sat yourself up in some cushy joint up here!"

I tapped the towering Inquisitor on his shoulder. "Sauers, the brand is Sauers, was being shipped out of a Richmond warehouse up until a few years ago."

The Inquisitor slapped me on the back. "My man!" and turned with venom on the Subject, "And that Helmans and Kraft shit proves you ain't from the South. The good mayo down there was named something else entirely," he said as he turned to me, and I placed the Stake into the Northern Boy's Fortunate heart, "Dukes, Dukes is the high end Southern mayonnaise."

Now defeated at the inquest, and found wanting in terms of Strength and Courage earned in the school of poverty, the small well-dressed fellow was patted on the back and welcomed back into the fraternity. Unlike the Floyd Money advocate he was not found guilty of promoting Mastery without Strength and Courage in service to the dollar, but of simply aspiring to a level of masculinity that they all admired.

Subject: William, A.K.A. Black Superman

If a patron in this bar used to be a card carrying member of the Black Panthers, it would have to be William. William was my source for the article ***On The Steps***. William sometimes wears a vest, and various very cool slouch hats and berets. He would have been a middle weight in his youth, is a small heavyweight now, and keeps a neatly trimmed beard and mustache. He walks with more confidence than any man in the bar, and I have seen him stay late into the night playing pool with young guys from West Baltimore. William has a lot of vested masculinity, and would flash angry eyes at anyone who would question his physicality. He makes no effort to leave with another man, as this is the type of practical herd instinct favored by women and whites for protection against the predators of the night. William and I are a lot alike, though he has a more assertive personality.

William always brings reading material and seems to be in a contest with Quinn over how many books a year they read. William will be quick to disparage light reading, favoring classics, including Faulkner. My first meeting with William was when I was drinking with a young lady and he came over and gave me the 'sissy white boy test' and said good naturedly enough, "You know that is my wife you are sitting with."

To react with anger would show a lack of confidence in my *Mastery*.

To reacted apologetically would show a lack of *Courage*.

To flinch and not immediately comeback with something would show a lack of my own regard for my physical *Strength*.

Having passed many such tests in the past, I responded, "In that case, I'll give her back as soon as I'm finished with her."

He laughed and slapped me on the back and walked off with a smile. The lady said, "How come they always expect whites to be afraid of them."

"Because most whites are afraid of blacks. The one thing about these older black guys is they want to interact with someone who is worth their time. There are a lot of tests they put each other through. In a white man what they despise is cowardice and stupidity. He was making sure that I wasn't just sitting back here because it was packed up front. He's halfway to considering me a white guy worth knowing. As soon as I bring a book in here, and he asks to see it and then starts quizzing me about the content, then I will have passed his test as a man."

"Men are weird!" she said.

William eventually quizzed me about every book he saw me read. I have seen him tutoring a few adult victims of public education on reading and content retention and on 'grasping the subtext.' So, William is like a cross between Quinn and Hawk, mixing two types of men that less educated or less experienced fellows admire, which makes him something of a lightning rod at times.

The Strange Coochy Inquest

The cop, whose name slips me, who is like William a football coach, once put William on the stand in front of three other patrons, and in his strident tone accused the Subject, "You mean to tell me that you would not take a young piece of pussy just because you were married."

"No I would not," said William in his soft tone.

"Bullshit! We were designed to want that pussy. Ain't no old ass man goin' to tell me that if a young piece of pussy come at him, that he is not going to be all over that."

"That may be your debased perspective, but I do not share it."

"Brother, you are full of shit. If a sweet young thing puts that strange coochy up on the table for you, you will not resist it—you are not designed to!"

"I have passed your test brother, and I will again, for the young women still desire me, as I am a man of substance."

That suave line brought a cussing fit from the cop, which is essentially an acknowledgment of defeat.

This is an apex inquest, the type that a man with recognized Strength and obvious Courage is put to; a direct test of his Honor. William made his point with a demonstration of his Mastery in conversation, meaning he pitched a shutout in this contest.

The Black Superman Inquest

When the riots in Fergusson Missouri erupted I noticed a black couple sitting next to the whites. She pointed at the TV in anger and he 'shushed' her not wanting to discuss racial politics in mixed company. Thinking this night would be a rare opportunity to observe a racial politics discussion I returned when the whites had drifted mostly off and the back of the bar was well stocked with men of this manly circle. I was speaking with Hawk about old time boxers.

The GQ Mugging Inquest

The men all agreed with the liberal media that the shooting of Tiny Teen by a white cop was a bad thing, with two exceptions: Hawk blew it off as 'some knucklehead bullshit,' and the cop, made the case for police in general, who are attacked by young men at an increasingly frequent rate. He said, "Look, we fear for our lives too. All we ask is that when we try to arrest you, that you don't do no stupid shit. Your goddamned lawyer is gonna' get your shit thrown out a court on Monday anyhow!"

William rose to accept the bait that had been so shrilly laid before him and declared, "If I am not wrong, I will not be arrested—will not stand for it."

"Is you stupid or crazy? You mean to tell me you gonna fight a cop?"

"If I am in the right, I will fight."

The cop just shook his head as if to say, "This man is going to get himself shot one day."

Quinn rose up as Assistant Inquisitor and said, "So, what are you, Black Superman—bullets bouncing off your chest? Are you crazy man?"

William opened his hands like Sitting Bull waiting for the Indian police to come murder him, amid the bemused laughter that greeted Quinn's real politic statement, "Characterize it as you will."

The Black Superman Inquest was a pure manly question that could not be fathomed by most women or most whites, namely the question of Honor, and whether or not a specific notion of Honor can be Honorably set aside in the face of overwhelming force. That Honor is of importance is alien to the feminized mind, as the feminist immersion in a purely material world precludes the consideration of transcendent values such as Honor. A sense of duty to the material order or a certain ideology is the best the feminized mind can generally muster for a surrogate to the truly spiritual concept of Honor. William was essentially making the case for transcendence over the values of the material order of Modernity. In their defense, his inquisitors were essentially arguing, that as 'spiritual inmates' of a material order, a purist sense of Honor is a trap that our temporal masters will use against us.

Subject: Quintin L. Tates

Quinn is a phys ed. teacher and tennis coach who publishes his own gratis newsletter THE BASELINE SPORTSPAGE under his TWENTY 5 PRODUCTIONS imprint. The content for the November 2014 issue includes an opinion piece on Ray Rice and the NFL spousal abuse scandals, two articles on the Baltimore Orioles baseball team, the feature on LeBron James' return to Ohio, and 'Dressing for Success: a look at the sartorial tastes on the tube,' in which he discusses men's fashion.

Below are some quotes from this 24 page zine

On Ray Rice: "Pretending that he never existed is equally offensive as what he did."

On Washington Redskins owner Daniel Snyder resisting NFL pressure to rename the team to appease Native American feminists from tribes alien to the Potomac Watershed, whose men would have gladly scalped their ancestors: "Not being a Skins fan I have no dog in this fight. But there is a part of me that says leave the name as it is. The Redskins emblem does not show a degrading image as its symbol."

Quinn told me a story about standing up to his father when he was a 195 pound college athlete. His father was a stern figure, so Quinn's nerves failed him and he grabbed a baseball bat defensively. This is how Quinn described the encounter as ending:

"He comes into my room and says, 'Are you going to hit me with that bat?'

"I said, 'Not unless you tell me to sir.'"

"That was my father. Kids today—by law—can't get that kind of schooling. Every guy I know has a story about standing up to his father, usually when he is around sixteen. It usually doesn't go to well. These were real men, not some absentee sperm donator. My favorite was my one friend who said he stood up to his dad—actually raised his hands to his father in the kitchen. His father could have punched him out—he's a grown ass man after all. But what he did was far better. He grabbed him by the hips and set him up on the refrigerator, and just went to bed."

So, that is a little about Quinn, the subject of the most Brutal Manly Inquest to be conducted at the Mixed Race Sports Bar.

The GQ Mugging Inquest

One Saturday afternoon I sat at the back corner of the long side of the bar with a lady to my right. Hawk sat three stools down on the long side. Two men closer to my age, who had played college basketball, sat between us. On the end, to my left, was an empty stool.

In walked Quinn in a suit and tie and an issue of Gentleman's Quarterly under his arm, in place of his typical coaching suit and tennis racquet case. I complimented Quinn as he asked me if I read GQ, touting it as a journal of note, and the tough white broad next to me whispered in my ear, "What the fuck, is that Cosmopolitan for Men, or what?"

Then Hawk chimed in, "We got a reckoning muthafuca!"

Quinn stood at momentary attention, having been called to account by the man's man in the bar like Fletcher Christian standing for a dressing down by William Bligh on the deck of The H.M.S. Bounty.

"What did I do?" he said to me out of the side of his mouth.

Hawk jumped on him with vitriol, "Muthafuca, don't be talkin' ta Jimmy unless you asking for a boxing lesson. Lord knows you never thrown a punch in your life. We need to settle this shit right here."

The GQ Mugging Inquest

As the GQ Mugging Inquest got formerly underway
the assembled jury nodded in agreement that it was
good day to run a well-dressed man through the
manly gantlet. I commented to Quinn, "If that's
what happens when you walk in here dressed like
that, I'm glad I threw out all my ties when I retired."

Quinn absently straightened the knot of his tie as he
sat for his grilling and said to me as he met his
Inquisitor's glare, "I know what this is about. Just
because a man is well-dressed does not make him
less of a man."

Hawk directed his attention to me, but his
accusatory finger toward the Subject of the inquest
at my side. "Jimmy, you know we got this stuff going
on with these hoodlums in the neighborhood. So I
look out. As I'm driving down the road the other
day, there's Quinn, strolling along—tennis racquet
and all, not a care in the world—got his self a little
buzz on."

Quinn attempts to interject a point and Hawk's girl
raises up from behind him [This, the tolerance of a
female opinion on the Inquisitor's side, means that
this was a manly issue of some gravity, like when
the Tuaregs let their women torture French Foreign

Legionnaires.] and shouts him down, "It ain't your turn!"

Quinn says tensely from the corner of his mouth, "Good Lord, we have Johnny Cochrane in drag up in here."

Hawk continues, "Now little does this GQ here know that three hoodlums got him in their sights."

Quinn rises to object and is shouted down by the lady, "Wait your turn Tennis Racquet."

Quinn sits down and groans, "Good Lord it's on now. I need a drink."

Hawk goes on, "Well Jimmy, I swerve over and get into the ramming lane—figure I'll clip one of these young hoppers but he bolts—spry as an alley cat up onto the curb. I stop and get out, ready to level another—I figure it's his responsibility to take out the third one. It is his mugging after all."

Quinn rises to make an objection and gets the hand from Hawk, "Muthafuca, don' even start on that 'Oh, I was loosening my racquet to take care of business' bullshit."

Quinn sat down with a groan, "Please just tell me when it's my turn."

I patted him on the shoulder seam of the well-tailored suit jacket and Hawk turned the Hand of Sit Down and Shut up into the pointed Finger of Accusation, and addressed me, "I'm tellin' you Jimmy, the man did not see it commin' and he should own up to it."

Quinn then stood and addressed the Inquisitor, "I'm not saying I saw them, or that I'm not grateful to you, just that I had a sense—"

Hawk dismissed his plea like a secular judge would dismiss a defendant's claim to 'ignorance of the law' with a sadly shaken head, unleashing the female terror at his side, who rose and pronounced sentence, "The glove don't fit!"

Hawk shook his head sadly as he bought me a drink and his lady shouted down Quinn, who, like the subject of the Mayo Sandwich Inquest, had been found wanting in some way, but was being made to feel it in a less convivial manner. As Quinn groaned Hawk whispered, "Jimmy, what am I going to do with him? He just don't get it."

The GQ Mugging Inquest

Quinn and I had a conversation about self-defense and avoidance tactics, which was why Hawk chose this moment to basically detail me to discuss street survival with his least 'street-minded' friend. The GQ magazine and the suit screamed 'Mug me, I might as well be white'. This impression was apparent to all but Quinn.

Like with the Floyd Money' Inquest, Hawk is very critical of men who focus more on Mastery than the basics of Strength and Courage. This was the subtext that was not brought up, as this inquest was intended to have some fun shocking Quinn into being more singular in his approach to avoidance. If this had been an attempt to embarrass him, which it was not, Hawk would have brought up the fact that Quinn makes it a habit [very sensible from a white perspective] of timing his leaving the bar with a friend who happens to be leaving in a car so he can get a lift home. Quinn had recently confided in me how nervous he was about these youths hunting him and others on the street. Hawk wants Quinn to eat the 'mayo sandwich' of street survival and develop a grit and cageyness that he regards as a necessity.

The GQ Mugging Inquest was a theatrical reminder by the group that the individual who stresses

Mastery at the expense of Strength and Courage risks having his Honor called into question.

A House Divided

I see much of modern media 'reporting' and political activism, from both the dominant Left and the reactionary Right, as a litany of divisive measures intended to keep men separated into warring camps in support of the various fears foisted upon our women by politicians and journalist. The most obvious attempt is the NFL's media witch hunt against any black man who might want to set his son up on the refrigerator.

I have had much negative to say about sports as a diversionary device to keep the populous compliantly distracted ***Bread And Circuses***. But the strength of sports in terms of keeping men together is that sports is one of the few areas where men of different racial and ethnic and political backgrounds can find common cause. The men in the bar I have described do not just discuss sports, but use sports as a means of discussing what is more important. In my crackpot opinion, what American men need is more mixed race sports bars where the feminist agenda of transforming every man except for active duty war fighters and cops into a quivering 'mangina' will find little traction.

There was a time when the word 'Sport' described a fellow who belonged to a classless and raceless society known as 'the sporting set' and before that in Britain as 'the fancy'. This 19th Century phenomenon was a reaction by poor men and the old land owning class to the new order or the world that was based on nothing but money, the rule of the industrialist and the businessman, and his risk-averse womanly concerns with posh comforts and monetary gain at the expense of anything and everything. I'd like to close out this writing year with a suggestion that a return of 'sportsmanship' in a role wider than that applied to athletic behavior might go a long way toward slowing the cultural rot around us.

Appendices

On The Steps

Urban Traditions: Body Punching & Sports as an Exit Option

Yesterday I had a wide-ranging interview with William: athlete, coach and army veteran, who moved to Baltimore from South Carolina in 1953. Eventually our discussion digressed into sports as a way out of the 1960s ghetto for boys of his generation. At this point he brought up something that has always intrigued me. Being a laborer working with mixed race crews most of my life, I was always intrigued by the difference in how black-on-black disputes and white-on-white disputes were resolved in very different ways. One of the unique aspects of the masculine black tradition was 'body-punching'; a type of limited on-the-job fight that very rarely escalated or resulted in a lingering animosity.

I'll let William tell it in his own words.

"The neighborhood was ordered around the steps, and your step 'rights'. You always had the right to sit your own steps. But sitting on other people's steps, or, most importantly, on corner or vacant steps, you did at the pleasure of the young men, the older respected teens.

"Body punching was an important aspect of this. Two boys would be set to fight by the teens, and you had your strike zone, belt to collar. That was all good. If you could not man up to this your were not allowed on the steps. And nobody really got hurt. If someone was just being overwhelmed it was broken up and you parted friends. There were no winners or losers. It was about standing up, being a man.

"Now, if you did something low down; vandalism, punch someone in the face, use a weapon, the older boys got you. Just a beating, that was just enough to get the point across, not to damage. Of course, that is abuse, a crime today. Now you have shooting and stabbing as choices that are optioned early on in the process of finding your way as a youth.

"Of course, coming into another neighborhood, the rules did not apply, and a fight that went beyond body-punching, and in which there was no guarantee that others would not jump in, was a real clear possibility.

"For a natural athlete, that three-in-ten guy, that guy who had what it took to make a go, this type of process prepared you well for a life of sports, which, considering the opportunities of those times, was the alternative to running from the police and getting caught up in all of that. Sports are still a real window of possibilities to the young man of the city, but it is just a window, a passing opportunity.

"I will never compete with another rec. program. Anyone who is working with youth should be honored and supported. It is also necessary to set up a filtering process, that permits high school and college coaches and recruiters to see the promising athletes, and also denies them direct early access; in other words, they must go through a parent and coach. And this, this waning of parental involvement in sports, has been detrimental.

"Football or baseball? You really have to ask which one I liked the most?

Laughs.

"That is easy: football. In baseball you are lucky to get your bat or glove on the ball in one of three plays. In football—I was a defensive back—I got to hit someone on every play."

Quinn's Walk

The Black 70s Survivor as a Postmodern Urban Crime Target

© 2014 James LaFond

Quinn is a 58 year old tennis coach. I was drinking with him at the bar a week ago, on a Sunday night, watching a good ball game. The ball game ended a little too late for his taste and he became nervous, watching the street for young black men patrolling for victims.

Quinn is a black man. Unlike the news media that reports only white on black violence, and the alternative online press that reports only black on white violence [which is 10 to 15 times more likely than white on black violence], Quinn and I know that most violent crime is black on black, at twice the rate as black on white.

He looks to me and confides, "I'm nursing this last beer, looking out the window, trying to time these kids. They have approached me on the bus stop before. At my age, sure, I can take down one. Then what happens they either swarm me and I go down, or they back off and I'm a criminal for attacking some mamma's poor baby. This walk is starting to drain my nerves. These aren't serious hood-rats or thugs, but kids with employed parents who vote and have political clout. They're like the rich white man's hoodlum boys from back in the day—looking for a good time and a reputation at a man's expense."

Quinn has recently discovered that I train fighters.

He turns to me and asks, "How do you deal with this. You look very unassuming—not like a fighter at all—you know the stereotype. Do people know about you, about your background?"

"I don't really regard myself as a dangerous person, particularly not unarmed. I practice avoidance. I never engage in arguments—ask any women I've been with. I just walk away. I have been studying the crimescape around here:

"The mixed race trio was broken up—literally—with a mallet earlier this year. The white guy that got his hands broken was the cohesive element, the scout. The drive up muggers—the men from the West Side—they only worked us here while the heat was on the BGF last year. The three vicious white boys that moved into the neighborhood are strictly criminal on criminal types—the corners are safe because of them. The kids you are worried about actually sit next to the ATM machine waiting. Sometimes they stake it out from the church. Their older associates hang at the gas station and are pretty much just a danger to stumbling drunks, hookers, crippled guys. They get high behind the church and wave to me when I walk by. I'm the local white trash dirt bag—like a mascot. They actually call me sir. I have used the ATM openly in front of them and motioned for them to follow me into the neighborhood and they just wave."

Quinn looked at me with a kind of eyebrow raised dread and said, "Jesus, I'll just get a lift. Hey Mister Al, can you give me a lift brother?"

Mister Al walked by in his suit and fedora with his pimp cane, shook my hand, and patted Quinn on the back. "I understand Son."

He then grinned at me as he guided Quinn off the stool with a fatherly hand, "This man would sell me swamp gas and call it ocean front property Jimmy.

But they don't make us like they used to and an old hand has to make sure these puppies get home safe."

I closed the bar with a giant hillbilly and 8 young black folks who looked to me to referee their argument over what constituted 'Eastside and Westside'. I pointed to the ancient hillbilly Nimitz Class hair carrier and said, "When you stop seeing white dudes that look like that and start seeing white guys that look like Russians [I did not want to explain what a Polish person was] or belong in a mobster movie, then you're on the Eastside. This is the Northeast."

What Awaits the Man Who Fails to Find His Way: Mo Coffee

Homeless in Harm City

© 2013 James LaFond

"I got a story ain't got no moral."

-Billy Preston

The Heartless Blogger

I was homeless for six weeks in 2003.

My new roommate Eric was homeless for about the same period earlier this year. [See Eric's Backpack below].

I have stepped over dozens of freezing homeless men, primarily in the late 1990s.

I have written 'The Case for The Panhandler Genocide.'

My column, 'Panhandler Nation' is largely a rant against the acquisitively homeless.

On the other hand I am a big fan of 17th Century pirates, Germanic nomad tribes, and Magyars, who were all essentially virulently covetous homeless folk.

So, what I am about to write may surprise you.

Beyond the Ghetto?

As a food market clerk, working for Good Guys R' Us out in the county, I pulled three shifts in a row leading up to Thanksgiving. I normally do not work even two nights in a row. This afforded me the opportunity to see a rare and melancholy drama unfold.

This slice of the suburbs, ten miles beyond the Harm City line, is no longer pristine; has become a ghetto annex, a target of slothful imminent domain. The postmodern ghetto is an ever-expanding phenomenon, hollowing out at its core to make way for urban homesteaders of the nearly wealthy class, even as the parasitic hood-rats scatter in pursuit of the receding civilization that is their reluctant host.

Our store has been open for 24 hours since January. Doing this in the ghetto is suicidal on many levels, but is workable, here, far beyond the criminal epicenter of our society. The night captain discussed the eventual homeless encroachment of winter earlier this year, dreading the consequences and his inequitable role in the store policies that would surely ensue.

Mo Coffee

On Monday night 11/25/13 I notice a black man in late middle-age, wearing slightly dirty sweats and old sneakers, limping through the store to the coffee pot. He is suffering from the onset of a nervous system disorder of some kind. He is very dark and has a droopy swollen lower lip. His appearance alone is enough to evoke pity. I have worked predominantly on majority black night crews throughout my life.

The GQ Mugging Inquest

I have noticed that dark-skinned men with large lips are often ridiculed by their peers. Even the big dangerous ones get picked on behind their back, so you know it had to be bad for this guy in childhood. I once worked with a multiple murderer with the street name of Mumblejack. This dude was super scary. Even so, the other black clerks would make fun of him constantly with sayings such as, "Dat nigga straight from Africa!" and "Sheee, dat nigga got lips bigga den Mick Jagga!"

I find much to pity about this man, particularly the fact that he is on the street during a blast of cruel winter weather. I also find some things to admire.

He keeps his purchases spread out to about one an hour and then takes his time consuming them on the bench up front. When he no longer has a legitimate purpose to be in the store he will pace out front on the sidewalk, staying out of the way of customers, and even cleaning up trash.

He never panhandles.

When Charlene bought him coffee, he thanked her, and did not come back to her again expecting a handout. He even wipes the counter around the coffee pot. When other customers are nearby, he makes himself scarce, not wanting to be a nuisance.

I take to calling him 'Mo Coffee' as he hits the pot every hour for the 13 hours I am on the job. He notices when we come up front on our breaks to sit, and goes outside during these times. This dude is the perfect homeless guy.

On Tuesday night, as I take my seat on the bench to finish reading V.J. Waks novel Hammerspace on my break, Bubba, our cashier, nods to Mo Coffee, and says, "You took his seat. He's going to stay outside in the cold until you're done."

Bubba comes over and leans on the back of the idle register lane. "He's a nice guy. It's kind of nice having him around. But you can see Reggie [the night captain] keeping an eye on him. How long do you think he'll be okay here?"

"He hit the jackpot. He is a low-impact specialist, the rare self-sufficient homeless guy. He has money. He spreads it out to make sure he's welcome or at least tolerated. He doesn't beg. He's a strong dignified man. Most of us would be crying in the gutter in his shoes, knocking on mom's door, begging for a space on the couch. He has survival protocols and sticks to them."

Bubba seems surprised that I am not calling for his homeless head, knowing that I had once been among the cruelest and least tolerant store managers in the area. He nods again, "So you think management will let him stay?"

"I would have bounced him out on Monday. I was a heat-seeking missile where loiterers were concerned. He's Daniel Boone—the polite pathfinder. We are the Indians. Management is the chiefs. The panhandlers, muggers and thieves that have chased him out of the ghetto, they are the white soldiers coming to rape and pillage. You have to kill the pathfinder or drive him off, or you get overwhelmed. Zero tolerance is the only defense. You can't solve the problem. You can just move it down the street. When I took that management job there was always a panhandler on duty, about a half-dozen a day. When I resigned there were none, but the Aldis down the street had a picket line out front. When the store was open for business every gap in the bars was covered by a dude I had bounced off my lot."

Bubba seems sad, "Happy days."

"That's what Reggie is dealing with. He's already upset about telling this dude to get lost next week, when it's even colder out."

Bubba seems to be weighing the social scheme of things, and whispers, with a long look at Mo Coffee, "I like having him around. He's a nice guy."

On Wednesday night, I asked Bubba, "Where's our man?"

"John [the store manager] put him out."

Bubba was noticeably depressed by the encroaching darkness of the world. I said what I could to assuage the 19-year-old, "At least he saved Reggie from the guilt."

Bubba nodded and said wistfully as we looked out into the icy night, "I hope he found a place, at least to eat Thanksgiving dinner."

"Amen brother."

www.ingramcontent.com/pod-product-compliance
Lightning Source LLC
Chambersburg PA
CBHW071355310526
45790CB00017B/889